Future Tech

The Future of Communication

Jun Kuromiya

T0386257

Lerner Publications ✦ Minneapolis

Lerner Publications Company
An imprint of Lerner Publishing Group, Inc.
241 First Avenue North
Minneapolis, MN 55401 USA

For reading levels and more information, look up this title at www.lernerbooks.com.

Main body text set in Adrianna Regular.
Typeface provided by Chank.

Library of Congress Cataloging-in-Publication Data

Names: Kuromiya, Jun, 1992– author.
Title: The future of communication / Jun Kuromiya.
Description: Minneapolis : Lerner Publications, [2021] | Series: Searchlight books : Future tech | Includes bibliographical references and index. | Audience: Ages 8–11. | Audience: Grades 2–3. | Summary: "New technologies such as augmented reality, brain-computer interfaces, and lifelike robots will change the way humans interact with one another and their environment. Discover how people will communicate and use technology in the future"— Provided by publisher.
Identifiers: LCCN 2019058466 (print) | LCCN 2019058467 (ebook) | ISBN 9781541597327 (library binding) | ISBN 9781728413792 (paperback) | ISBN 9781728400808 (ebook)
Subjects: LCSH: Telecommunication—Forecasting—Juvenile literature. | Telecommunication—Technological innovations—Juvenile literature. | Artificial intelligence—Social aspects—Juvenile literature.
Classification: LCC TK5102.4 .K87 2021 (print) | LCC TK5102.4 (ebook) | DDC 303.48/330112—dc23

LC record available at https://lccn.loc.gov/2019058466
LC ebook record available at https://lccn.loc.gov/2019058467

Manufactured in the United States of America
1-47836-48276-2/24/2020

Contents

Chapter 1

NEW WAYS TO COMMUNICATE

Humans communicate in ways no other animal can. We have thousands of languages and express complex ideas. Art, math, science, music, and literature are all ways that humans communicate with one another. But in the years to come, cutting-edge technology will transform how we connect with people and with machines. The future of communication will make our lives easier, keep us healthier, and even allow us to read one another's minds.

Art can express an artist's mood, share an opinion, or tell a story.

Talking to Bots

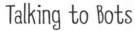

Through most of human history, we communicated only with one another and, using simple commands, with animals such as dogs and horses. Recently, we began communicating with computer programs and high-tech devices. As communication technology improves, talking to machines might become as common as talking to other people.

People use voice commands to interact with phones and other modern digital devices.

We already communicate a great deal with bots. These computer programs operate on their own. Usually we don't even notice them. They often run in the background, making sure websites and digital devices work the way they're supposed to. Bots create keywords for web pages. The keywords help internet users find recipes, articles, or anything else they're looking for.

YOU MAY NOT NOTICE BOTS ONLINE, BUT MOST WEB PAGES WOULDN'T WORK WITHOUT THEM.

As chatbot technology improves, the computer programs may replace most human customer service agents.

Companies use special bots called chatbots to interact with people. Customers communicate with chatbots through voice or text commands. Chatbots can understand what people want and respond like a human customer service agent would. Chatbots answer questions, provide instructions, and help customers navigate websites. Unlike human workers, chatbots are always available to help. Bots never sleep, and they can help many customers at the same time.

People access virtual assistants through tabletop speakers, phones, and computers.

Some of the technology we use every day needs bots to work. People use virtual assistants such as Alexa and Siri on phones and other devices. When you ask Alexa for directions, a restaurant review, or a weather report, a bot provides the results.

With bots, virtual assistants make devices a lot easier to use. That's a big advantage for people who are unfamiliar with digital technology or have special needs. With simple voice or text commands, a bot can order food, call a friend, and write an email. Bots allow more people to access modern technology.

Voice-controlled virtual assistants make internet access easy for people who didn't grow up using digital devices.

Companies are developing self-driving vehicles like this bus for widespread public use.

Smart Bots

Bots soon will be able to do much more than simple chores. With artificial intelligence (AI), they could become bus drivers, teachers, and even doctors. Like all bots, they won't need to sleep, eat, or take breaks. More important, they'd be less likely to make mistakes than human drivers and doctors would. That could save people's lives.

Bots provide many advantages, but their widespread use raises new challenges too. Some people might not feel comfortable talking to a bot doctor. Bot drivers and teachers will fill jobs that humans had, forcing people to seek different work. As AI technology improves and bots become more common, we must think carefully about their role in society.

> To get the best medical care, patients must communicate openly with their doctors.

Chapter 2

READING MINDS

Have you ever wished you could know what someone is thinking? What about sending thoughts straight from your brain to someone else's? These amazing ideas might be possible sooner than you think. Scientists are developing high-tech ways for people to send messages between brains.

Mind reading has always been an invention of science fiction. But modern technology could make this fantasy a reality.

It takes highly specialized gear, such as this cloth cap with sensors, to record electrical brain activity.

In one experiment, scientists connected two people to a special device with sensors that recorded the electrical activity of their brains. Using just their thoughts, the people were able to send instructions to each other through the device. One day, mind-reading technology may be available to everyone.

STEM Spotlight

Researchers at Massachusetts Institute of Technology are developing a device that can detect emotions. The device reads people's heart rates and determines their feelings based on heart rate changes. It can detect emotions such as anger, sadness, and excitement. Emotion-detecting technology of the future could help companies judge the popularity of new products. A home device might play calming music when you're angry or call a friend when you're sad.

When you're angry, your breathing and heart rates rise.

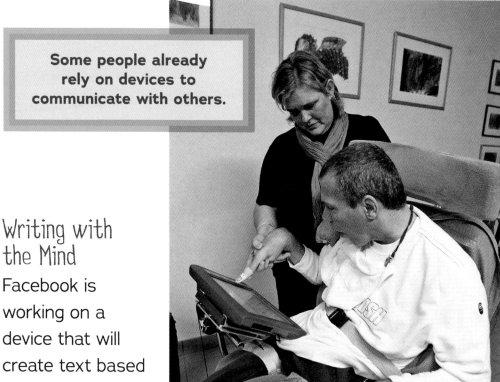

Some people already rely on devices to communicate with others.

Writing with the Mind

Facebook is working on a device that will create text based on a person's thoughts. It records electrical brain activity produced when someone thinks certain words and then attempts to translate and display the words on a screen. This technology will give some people who are unable to speak a way to communicate quickly and easily. Using the device, they could express their thoughts in real time.

To get precise readings of the brain's electrical activity, sensors must be directly connected to the head. In some experiments, scientists attach sensors to the surface of the head. But in others, researchers insert wires into the skull or even directly into the brain!

TO GET ACCURATE BRAIN DATA, RESEARCHERS USE SENSORS, WIRES, AND MONITORS.

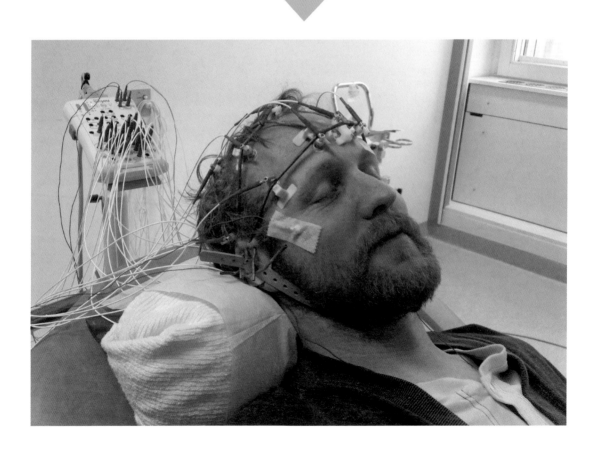

Scientists are working on wireless devices for everyday use that will record electrical activity in the brain and translate it. Such technology could allow two people wearing the devices to communicate with each other just by thinking. One day we may be sending thought messages instead of text messages.

Wearable brain sensors for everyday use could lead to big changes in the ways we communicate.

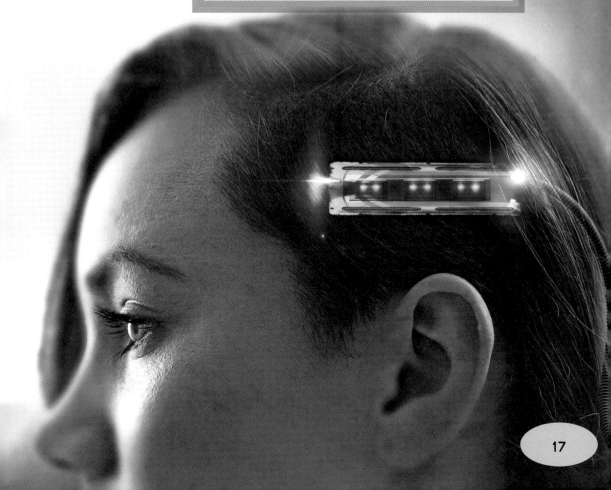

Chapter 3

LANGUAGE EVOLUTION

Around the world, scientists and engineers are inventing new communication technology every day. How we talk to one another is rapidly changing. For example, modern technology has introduced a huge range of new words into human languages. Terms such as podcast, blog, and virtual reality are recent inventions designed to

As engineers design new communication technology, people create new words to describe it.

Trolls try to offend people with their words and posts.

describe modern technology. In 2018, Merriam-Webster's Dictionary added more than one thousand words.

Meanwhile, some old words have taken on new meanings. A troll is a creature from folklore that usually lives in caves or under bridges. As social media grew in popularity, *troll* became a common term for people who criticize and harass others online. Then the word evolved again to include people who cause trouble off-line.

EVERY DAY, BILLIONS OF PEOPLE USE THE INTERNET TO SHARE IDEAS, TELL STORIES, AND EXPLORE THE WORLD.

Internet technology is the main reason for this rapid language change. It can instantly connect people around the world, allowing us to exchange new words and meanings incredibly fast. The internet reaches nearly every corner of the planet, causing language to evolve faster than ever before.

The Future of Ew!

If you wish you could smell what's on your screen when you're online, you're not alone. A group in Malaysia is creating smells electronically with a process that includes sticking wires up people's nostrils. When the technology improves, customers might get to smell a restaurant's meals when they check its menu online. Then again, you could also find nasty smells on the internet such as garbage, skunks, and someone's stinky breath.

With digital smell technology, computers could produce the scent of garbage.

Translation Machines

Companies are developing devices that will instantly translate speech into a wide range of languages. As people speak, the machines will translate the speech into words users can understand. This technology will help international travelers and businesspeople who go to many different parts of the world.

Translation software could help people who speak different languages complete complex business deals.

Around the world, people speak about seven thousand different languages.

Instant translation technology has many benefits, but it could also lead to the loss of thousands of languages. If people rely on translation software, they won't need to learn as many languages. Languages with fewer speakers could die out completely. Some experts predict we could lose up to 90 percent of modern languages.

Chapter 4

COMMUNICATION AND PRIVACY

As communication technology gets better, it has the potential to improve our lives in several ways. Bots and virtual assistants will manage our routine shopping needs, giving us more free time. People with problems speaking will have new ways to express themselves. We may even be able to communicate with just our thoughts.

As digital technology improves and makes our lives more convenient, we rely on it more and more.

Internet data is stored in servers around the world. All the information people put online exists in a computer somewhere.

But cutting-edge communication technology has possible drawbacks too. It will make it harder to do or say things privately, especially if the ability to read thoughts and emotions improves and becomes widespread. Our virtual assistants will know almost everything about us, from what we eat to the medicines we take and the TV shows we watch. That could leave us open to potential attacks from hackers and others.

Sharing Our Personal Lives

For most people, personal privacy is extremely important. We choose what we share with other people, and we have the freedom to keep our thoughts

to ourselves. But imagine if your friends or classmates could know all your thoughts and feelings. Advanced technology could make that more likely. Would you want to share your feelings with your teacher? What about a stranger?

Some cities, such as London, England, have hundreds of thousands of cameras to record people on streets, at famous landmarks, and in other public places.

With public cameras, sensors, and data from personal devices, governments can gather huge amounts of information about their citizens.

Hackers and government officials could gain access to data about your thoughts and emotions. The government of China has developed a system for people to earn social credit by behaving in ways the government wants. The system is designed to guard against bad business practices. Someday, such a system could be used to reward and punish people for what they think and how they feel.

Some facial recognition technology works by measuring distances between facial features, such as the distance between the eyes and the nose.

Facial and fingerprint recognition technology could also help governments and hackers gain access to your information. Recognition software is used in phones and other communication gear. It allows devices to identify people by reading their faces and fingerprints. Governments and hackers could track where we go and what we do.

The future of communication is exciting and full of possibilities. As we rely more and more on communication technology, the flow of information between people, machines, and governments will increase. To avoid misuse of this data, we must answer big questions about privacy and how we interact with people in our communities and around the world. If we get the answers right, communication technology could improve the lives of everyone on Earth.

Engineers and designers will keep inventing new ways for people to communicate and connect.

Glossary

artificial intelligence (AI): a computer program or machine that can express intelligent human behavior

bot: a computer program that performs automatic tasks

chatbot: a bot designed to communicate with people

digital: electronic and computer technology

folklore: traditional tales, sayings, dances, or art forms that people preserve

hacker: someone who illegally breaks into a computer system to access its data

keyword: an important word from a title or document that is used to find content

recognition: the act of sensing something or someone previously known

sensor: a device that responds to heat, light, or movement

translate: to turn into one's own or another language

virtual: being on a computer or computer network

Learn More about the Future of Communication

Books

Brezina, Corona. *Artificial Intelligence and You*. New York: Rosen, 2020. Read about artificial intelligence and how it will be used in the future.

Hubbard, Ben. *My Digital Community and Media*. Minneapolis: Lerner Publications, 2019. Learn how the internet and social media shape our communities.

Lyons, Heather. *Coding to Create and Communicate*. Minneapolis: Lerner Publications, 2018. Learn more about digital communication, and try out fun coding activities.

Websites

Artificial Intelligence Facts for Kids
https://kids.kiddle.co/Artificial_intelligence
Find out about the history of artificial intelligence and how it will change in the future.

How Language Began
https://online.kidsdiscover.com/unit/language/topic/how-language -began-5-theories
Explore the origins of human language.

Online Safety Tips
https://www.connectsafely.org/safetytips/
Learn how to stay safe online and protect your privacy.

Index

Photo Acknowledgments

Image credits: Witthaya Prasongsin/Getty Images, p. 4; LumiNola/Getty Images, p. 5; basketman23/Getty Images, p. 6; Atstock Productions/Shutterstock.com, p. 7; eyecrave/Getty Images, p. 8; kate_sept2004/Getty Images, p. 9; CHRISTOF STACHE/AFP/Getty Images, p. 10; Atstock Productions/Shutterstock.com, p. 11; KDdesignphoto/Shutterstock.com, p. 12; fotografixx/Getty Images, p. 13; Sergio Mendoza Hochmann/Getty Images, p. 14; STRINGER/AFP/Getty Images, p. 15; Marcus Leidner/EyeEm/Getty Images, p. 16; Colin Anderson Productions pty ltd/Getty Images, p. 17; Tom Werner/Getty Images, p. 18; Gorodenkoff/Shutterstock.com, p. 19; imaginima/Getty Images, p. 20; Jenny Dettrick/Getty Images, p. 21; ad_doward/Getty Images, p. 22; ferrantraite/Getty Images, p. 23; Tim Robberts/Getty Images, p. 24; Mischa Keijser/Getty Images, p. 25; Westend61/Getty Images, p. 26; DuKai photographer/Getty Images, p. 27; John M Lund Photography Inc/Getty Images, p. 28; Donald Iain Smith/Getty Images, p. 29.

Design elements: Patra Kongsirimongkolchai/EyeEm/Getty Images.

Cover image: John MacDougall/Getty Images.